Dinah the Aspie Dinosaur

The adventures and misadventures of a
young dinosaur with Asperger's Syndrome

Chloë Asper

For the doctors L. and L., who set me on my path to Aspie self-discovery, and for my Internet friends, with whom the meeting place may be virtual but for whom my feelings are very real.

Introduction

I was diagnosed with Asperger's Syndrome (high-functioning autism) in 2014, after many months of doing the rounds of various doctors and counsellors with mystery anxiety and depression, and a lifetime of being a little bit odd, feeling that I had somehow failed to read the user manual for life with which everyone else had been issued.

Over this time, I learned two things. The first is that knowledge is power. As someone autistic, once you are aware that your brain is not wired like the majority of people's, you can stop fighting it. Instead, you can make adaptations and take steps to work with it, and make life easier for yourself. The second thing that I learned, and perhaps the more important, is that laughter really is quite often the best medicine. In my opinion, sometimes the only reasonable way to handle a difficult situation is to laugh at it.

This is how Dinah the Aspie Dinosaur came to be; each of these comics is based on something that has happened to me in real life. I hope that Dinah may offer to the non-Aspie a small insight into the challenges of her everyday life, and to her fellow Aspies and auties, solidarity, and reassurance that they are not alone!

Dinah the Aspie Dinosaur and the Waiting Room

2

Dinah the Aspie Dinosaur and the Smartphone GPS

Dinah the Aspie Dinosaur and the Questionnaire

Dinah the Aspie Dinosaur and the Walk to Work

Dinah the Aspie Dinosaur and the Doctor Appointment

Dinah the Aspie Dinosaur and the Coffee Shop

Dinah the Aspie Dinosaur and the Sunglasses

Dinah the Aspie Dinosaur and the Evening Plans

Dinah the Aspie Dinosaur and the Waiting Room (2)

Dinah the Aspie Dinosaur and the Self-Appointed Autism Expert

Dinah the Aspie Dinosaur and the Library

12

Dinah the Aspie Dinosaur and the Unusual Greeting

13

Dinah the Aspie Dinosaur's Handy Phrasebook

Dinah the Aspie Dinosaur and Passport Control

Dinah the Aspie Dinosaur and the Conference Guest

Dinah the Aspie Dinosaur and the Optician

17

Dinah the Aspie Dinosaur and the Unexpected Visitor

Dinah the Aspie Dinosaur and the Illogical Bystanders

Dinah the Aspie Dinosaur and the Full Moon

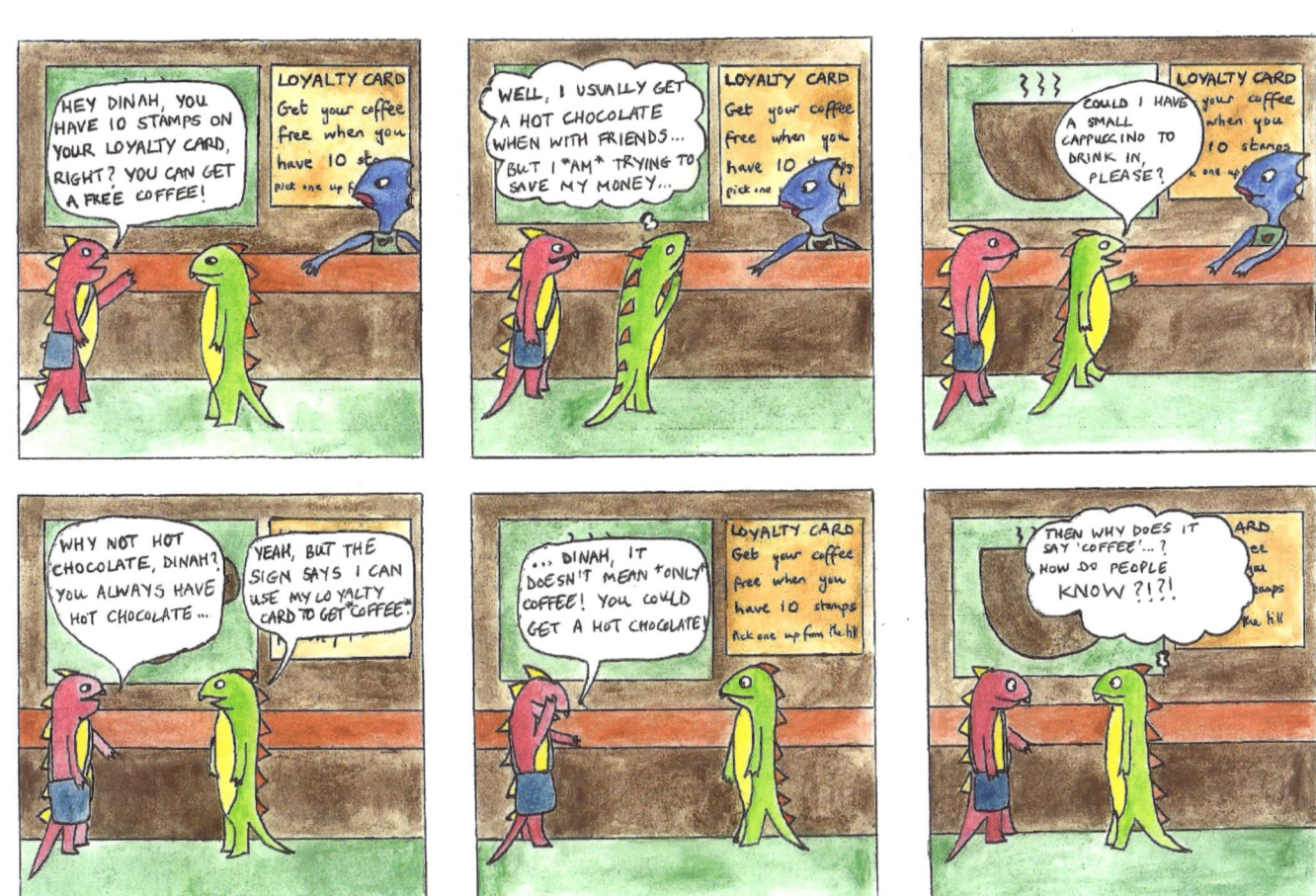

Dinah the Aspie Dinosaur and the Coffee Shop (2)

Dinah the Aspie Dinosaur and the Cinema

Dinah the Aspie Dinosaur and the Electrician

Dinah the Aspie Dinosaur and the Walk

Dinah the Aspie Dinosaur and the Effective Remedy

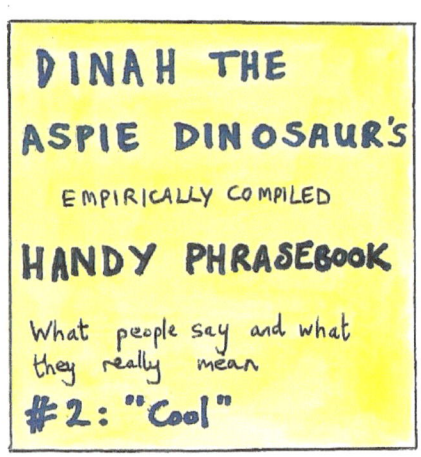

Dinah the Aspie Dinosaur's Handy Phrasebook (2)

26

Dinah the Aspie Dinosaur and the E-mail Salutation

Dinah the Aspie Dinosaur and the Phone Call

Dinah the Aspie Dinosaur and the Superpower

Dinah the Aspie Dinosaur and the Voicemail

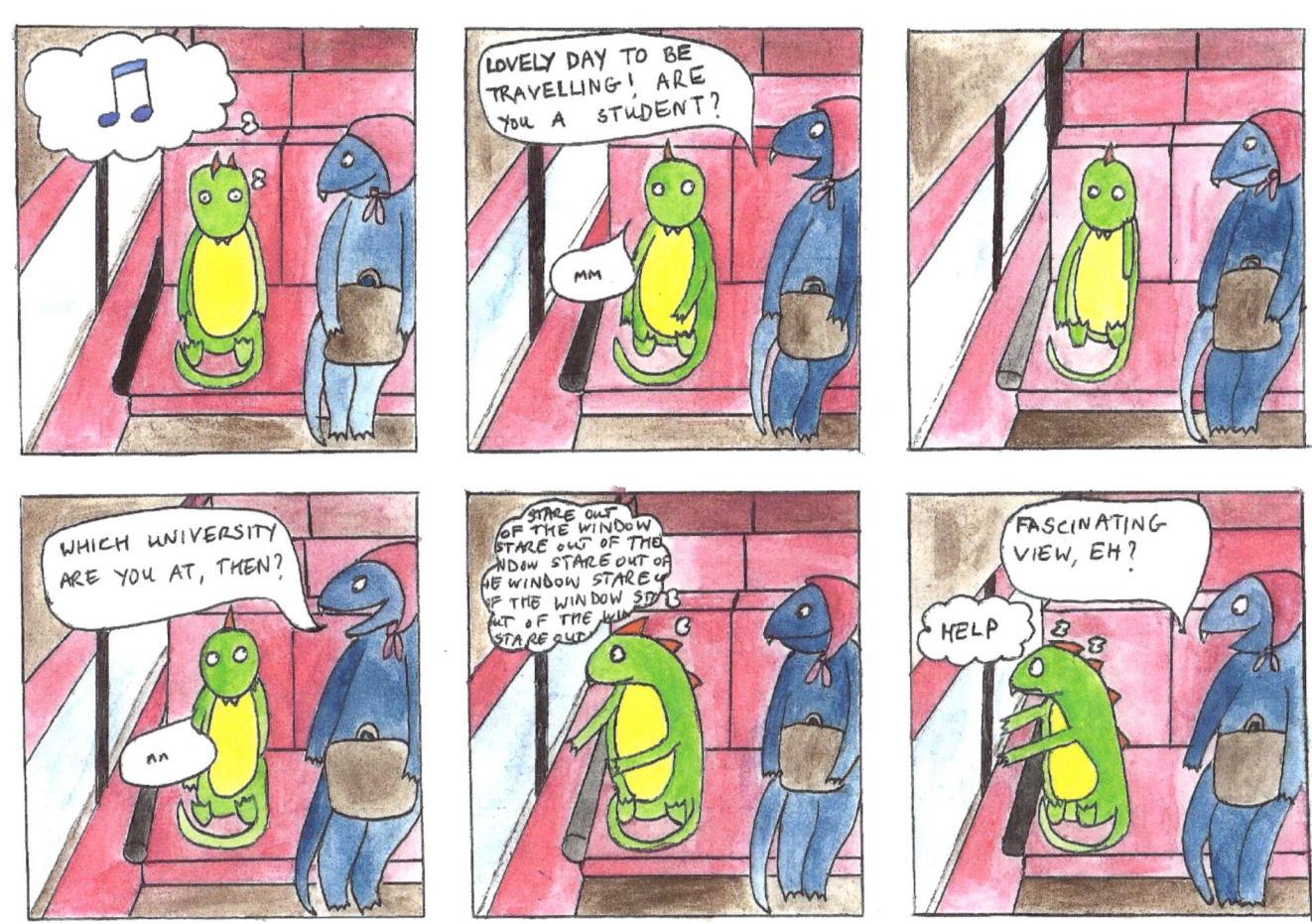

Dinah the Aspie Dinosaur and the Talkative Passenger

Dinah the Aspie Dinosaur and the Restaurant

32

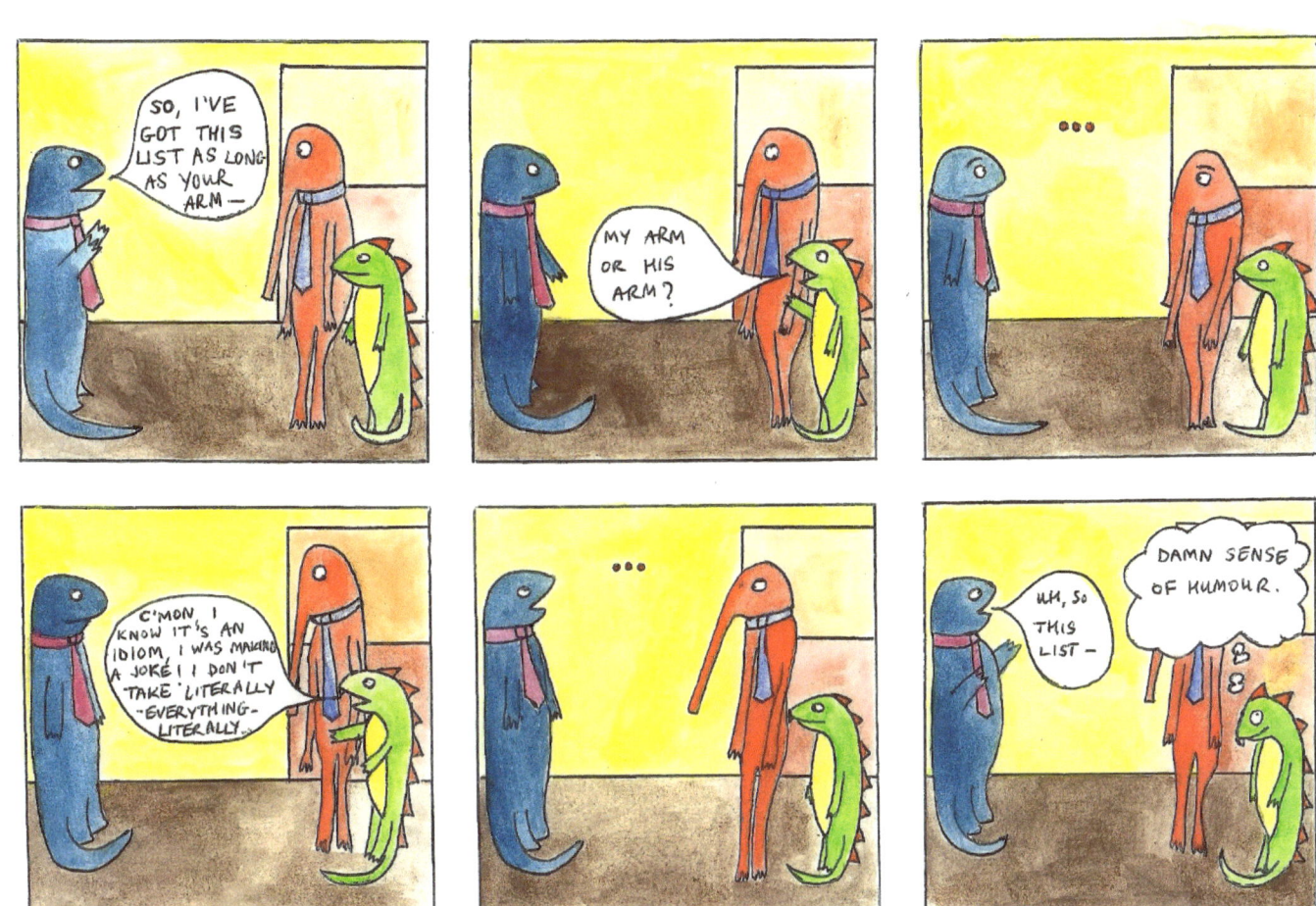

Dinah the Aspie Dinosaur and the Idiom

Dinah the Aspie Dinosaur and the Well-Meant Comment

Dinah the Aspie Dinosaur and the Coffee Break Chat

Dinah the Aspie Dinosaur and the Difficult Decision

Dinah the Aspie Dinosaur and the Doctor Appointment (2)

37

Dinah the Aspie Dinosaur and the Teaspoon

Dinah the Aspie Dinosaur and the Sandwich

Dinah the Aspie Dinosaur and the E-mail Reply

Dinah the Aspie Dinosaur and the Shopping Trip

Dinah the Aspie Dinosaur and the Online Social Network

Find Dinah the Aspie Dinosaur on:

Facebook: http://www.facebook.com/DinahTheAspieDinosaur

Twitter: @AspieDinoDinah

Wordpress: http://DinahTheAspieDinosaur.wordpress.com

www.ingramcontent.com/pod-product-compliance
Lightning Source LLC
Chambersburg PA
CBHW041518280526
45792CB00004B/1300